MAKE THIS JOURNAL!

My Bar / Bat Mitzvah Year

by _____
(your name here)

(with Ann D. Koffsky)

BEHRMAN HOUSE

For Eva and Rachelie in honor of their Bat Mitzvot.
(And for Ellie, too!)

-AK

The publisher gratefully acknowledges the following sources of images:

Cover: Shutterstock: Krasovski Dmitri (tape), Kostiantyn Kravchenko (pencil), Memory Stockphoto (paper)

INTERIOR: Shutterstock: Shtonado 4, 5, 18, 52; Lightkite 2; donatas1205 4; yokosung 10, 24, 44, 74; mhatzapa 11; tsaplia 12; Hand Kano 16, 20; michlomop 20, 21, 62, 63; lineartestpilot 22, 30, 71; Natasha Pankina 23; curiosity 24; 1001holiday 24, 27; miloge 25; Eloku 28; En min Shen 29, 42; Skokan Olena 31, 58, 64, 68, 81; Dmitry Zimin 32; RedHead_Anna 33; Magdalena Kucova 34, 37, 38, 57, 60, 72, 79, 85, 86; RaZZeRs 43; Ermak Oksana 48, 49 ,62, 63, 65; vgeniya Mukhitova 53; Mjosedesign 56; Nipatsara Bureepia 64; bingo_flamingo 77; Flipser 78, 79; nikiteev_konstantin 84; johavel 87; Halene 91; Finevector 94; zsooofija 96. Terry Taylor: 9, 21, 35, 40, 50.

Project Editors: Dena Neusner & Ann D. Koffsky

Designer: Terry Taylor Studio

Copyright © 2017 Behrman House, Inc.

Springfield, NJ 07081

ISBN: 978-0-87441-832-3

Printed in the United States of America

So, you're going to be a bar/bat mitzvah. **Mazel tov!** You're in for a fun, crazy, meaningful, stressful, spiritual, and oftentimes ridiculous year—you'll definitely want to remember it! We've made this journal to help.

By the end of your bar/bat mitzvah, this book will be a personal memento that you'll save and treasure. Or it will be a pile of blank pages. It's entirely up to you. It's kind of like the bar/bat mitzvah itself: what you put into it is what you'll get out of it.

So congrats! Enjoy the ride. Enjoy the family, the friends, the party. And may your bar/bat mitzvah be just the beginning of your happy, successful, and Jewishly meaningful life.

—Ann

*Note: Since we have never met you, we don't know if you are having a bar mitzvah or a bat mitzvah. As you go through this journal, you'll notice that we wrote "bar/bat." Just go with it, and circle the one that's right for you. You can start with the one on the cover. OK? Thx.

Write your full name in **HUGE** bubble letters.

Inside the letters, tell the story of why it's your name.

Draw two lines across this WHO-O-L-E page,

Make the top a timeline of your life until now.

one on **TOP** and one on the **BOTTOM**.

Add dots to both.

Make the second a timeline of this year, starting today.

Draw diagonal lines to divide this page into sections. In each section, write a different way you ID yourself (like your email address, social media name, username, nicknames, texting name or app names).

Write your name that you'll be called at your ceremony in synagogue. Use Hebrew letters. Decorate each letter in a different

Make three rectangles on this page. Fill each with a list of your faves (videos, YouTubers, sports, desserts, songs—whatever).

Make three ZIGZAGGY shapes on this page.
Fill them with lists of stuff you totally dislike.

Draw what you see outside your bedroom window.

Draw an overhead floor plan of your room.

Circle the spot you like the most.

Write a top 10 list called "Things I have done and am proud of."

1. _____

2. _____

3. _____

4. _____

5. _____

6. _____

7. _____

8. _____

9. _____

10. _____

Draw a big circle, with clock numbers around it. Write what you do on a school day next to each hour mark.

Trace your hand. On each finger, write a word that most describes your personality.

Draw a grid. Then make a word search of the names of your parents, grandparents, and ancestors.

Draw a star.
Fill it in with a
description of the
BEST thing
that ever
happened to you.

Draw an ugly shape. Fill it in with a description of the **WORST** thing that's ever happened to you.

Trace the hands of everyone who lives in your house.

Pets included!

Write an evite to someone who has passed away, inviting him or her to your bar/bat mitzvah.

Hold this journal on its side. Write your initials on the edges.

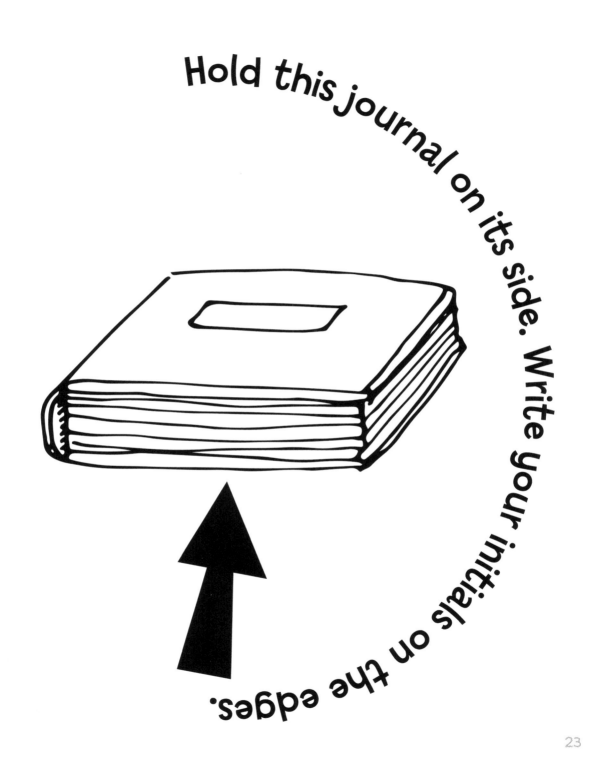

Write your **BIGGEST** *fears* about your bar/bat mitzvah here.

Then neatly cut this page out of the journal and shred it to pieces.

teachers, and other non-family people you are connected to on each of the swirls.

Write your name in the middle of this page and surround it with swirls. Write the names of your friends,

Staple photos of two people who have made a
POSITIVE IMPRESSION on you.
Add captions describing how they impressed you.

Write yourself a note of encouragement. Neatly cut it out and hang it
with your suit/dress so you'll see it on your big day.

Draw a flip-book animation of something that makes you smile on the corners of this journal.

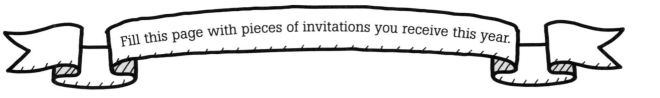

Fill this page with pieces of invitations you receive this year.

Write six instructions to an alien about how to be a good bar/bat mitzvah guest.

MAZEL TOV

1. _____

2. _____

3. _____

4. _____

5. _____

6. _____

COLLECT
the number
13
wherever
YOU
find it.

or **12**,
if that's when you
are celebrating
your bar/bat mitzvah.

_____

_____

_____

_____

_____

_____

_____

_____

_____

_____

_____

_____

_____

_____

_____

_____

Pretend your Torah portion *(parashah)* is a movie. Write up a blurb review of it for a website.

Sing a line of your Torah reading or prayer. As you do, close your eyes and draw a line on this page that reflects the notes that you sing.

33

that are most important

Draw pictures of things

to you all around it.

Paste a
photo of
yourself
here.

WRITE the name of a mitzvah that you like to do here and then one that you like better on top of that. Keep going until you reach the top of the page.

What are some BIG questions you have about being Jewish? Draw HUGE question marks and write your questions around them.

Fill these pages with pictures and words that describe what you like about being Jewish.

like. Add your own words to the prayer. Draw in the margins what it means to you.

Paste a copy of a prayer from the Shabbat service that you like to this page. Decorate the words that you

Draw

a

ladder.

Write

on each

rung

something

you would

like to do

before you

are bar/bat

mitzvah.

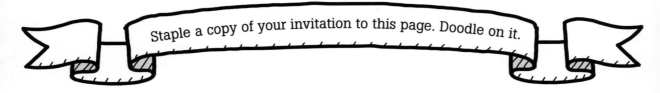

Staple a copy of your invitation to this page. Doodle on it.

Take a selfie in your bat mitzvah dress/
bar mitzvah suit, and tape it here.

Make a collage from the
response cards you get
(print them out if they
came back digitally).

Fill this page with clouds. Inside each one, write something that you want to remember from this year.

Write here what you **REALLY** would want to say in your bar or bat mitzvah speech, except there is no way your parents/rabbi would let you.

Paste the
first draft
of your speech here.

Circle what got cut.

Paste the
final draft
of your speech here.

<u>Underline</u> what got added.

Draw balloons flying in the sky across this page. In each balloon, write the name of someone who is helping you make your party (photographer, musicians, party planner . . .).

50

Draw or describe something you really want to include as part of your celebration but it's just too expensive.

Tweet your bar/bat mitzvah speech here (write it out in no more than 140 characters).

of the home page of two **websites** you like to visit.

On your birthday this year, take a **screenshot**

Print and staple them to this page.

Write
anything
that is
really

you on
this page.

Draw random shapes on this page. Fill in some of them with your theme colors. Fill in others with pictures relating to your theme.

Draw or describe something that someone in your family cares **A LOT** about for your party but you couldn't **care less** about.

Hold three pens together. Then write the name of your Torah portion (*parashah*) all over the page until it is full.

Draw a box in the middle of this page, and describe your mitzvah project inside the box. Add words, websites, and pictures that relate to your mitzvah project around the box.

Ask your parents to write a bar/bat mitzvah wish to you and what they hope for your future.

*Note: Tell them you love them too and that they should try not to cry while they write it.

WISH you could have as the food at your party.

Draw a giant plate and a fork and knife next to it. Collect pictures of the food that you

Fill this
page with
happy
thoughts.

Write a product review describing the most ridiculous bar/bat mitzvah idea that someone suggested to you.

(Leave some room, you might hear some more before the year is up!)

Draw a floor plan and label where friends, family, and your rabbi and cantor will be sitting when you are giving your speech.

WRITE the name of EVERYONE on your GUEST List.

But don't check the actual guest list first—see who you can remember.

Scribble WILDLY on this page when you are really STRESSED out.

Draw an envelope, with a stamp in the corner.

Address it to a person from Jewish history who you wish could come to your bar/bat mitzvah.

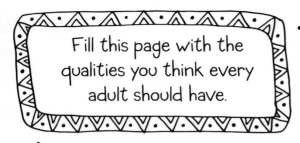

Fill this page with the qualities you think every adult should have.

Describe in excruciating detail the most boring thing you had to do to prepare for your bar/bat mitzvah.

Now write the name of every famous person you'd like to meet along the lines.

Draw stick figures of yourself as a baby, on your first day of school, and at your bar/bat mitzvah.

Draw a
picture of the

BEST

gift you have
ever been
given before
this year. Say
why you liked
it in three
words.

76

Draw

a big box with a bow on top. Inside, list some of the gifts you have gotten this year.

Around the box, write the names of people who gave you the gift and match them up with swirly lines.

Cover this page using scraps of wrapping paper from the presents and cards you get this year.

1 Write the website of a charity that you believe in.

2 Are you getting any $$$ gifts? Use the space in this box to list and add them up.

3 Calculate 10% of what you received and write that number here:

4 Consider donating that sum to your cause.

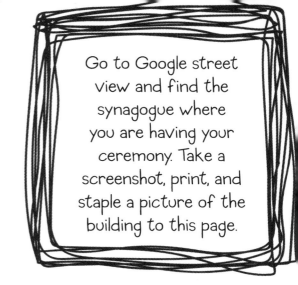

Go to Google street view and find the synagogue where you are having your ceremony. Take a screenshot, print, and staple a picture of the building to this page.

Staple
a copy of
the first thank-
you note that
you messed
up and
couldn't
send
here.

Write the **first** line of
the **first** prayer in your
ceremony's service.

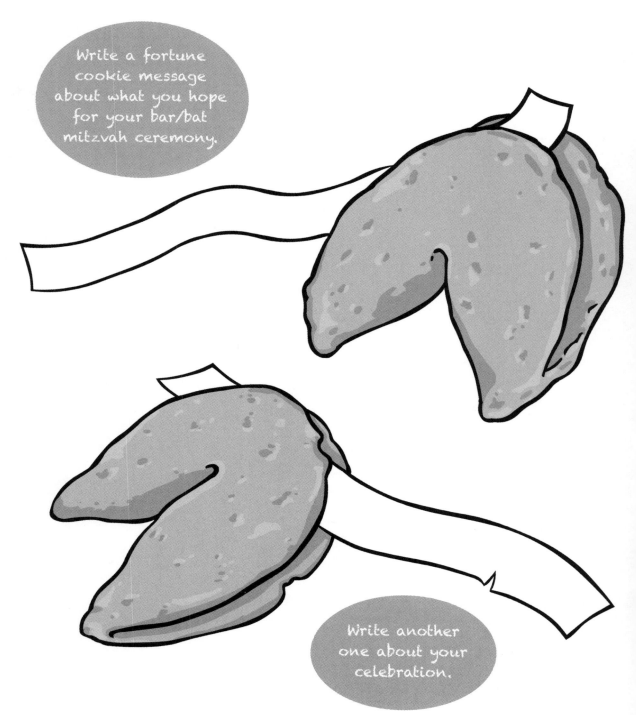

Take a piece of
your centerpiece
and paste it here.

Take a picture of your photographer(s) and paste it here. Just because, hey, it's their turn.

List all the places and countries you'd love to travel to.

Answer in five words or less:

If you could travel back in time to when you were 5, what would you tell your younger self to MAKE SURE to do?

_____

_____

_____

_____

_____

_____

_____

_____

_____

To make sure NOT to do?

Answer in five words or less:

If you could travel forward in time to when you are 85, what memory from this year would you remind your older self of?

Draw a staircase. Write on each step something you would like to do before you go to college.

Imagine a webzine profiles you on your 50th birthday. What would be the first sentence?

Of all the things you are learning this year, what do you think will be **MOST USEFUL** to you as you grow up? **LEAST USEFUL?**

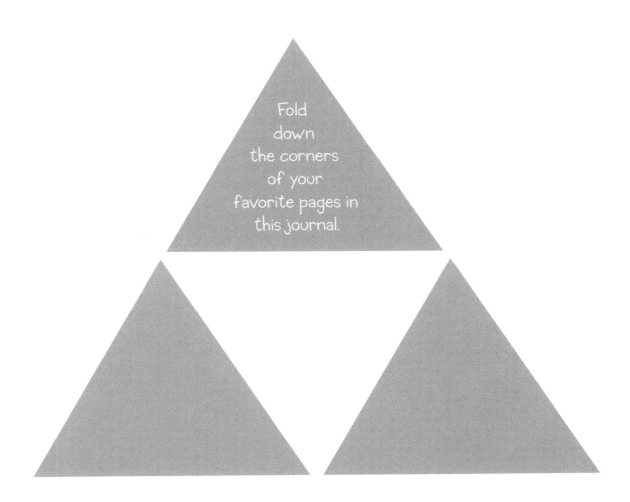

Fold
down
the corners
of your
favorite pages in
this journal.

Thank You!

Write a thank-you note to your parents for making you this shindig. Then neatly cut it out and give it to them.

Fill the
LEFT
side with
things
that went
perfectly
at your
bar/bat
mitzvah
celebration.

Fill the
RIGHT
side with what
went wrong.

Write a list of thirteen more things that we should have included in this journal.

1. _____

2. _____

3. _____

4. _____

5. _____

6. _____

7. _____

8. _____

9. _____

10. _____

11. _____

12. _____

13. _____

the end